**What They Said***:

'This book is so great, so good'
*Muhammad Ali*

'It trembles on the brink of obscenity'
*Lord Longford*

'Dull, it isn't' *The Metropolitan Police*

'Is this a book that you would ever wish your wife or servants to read?'
*Mervyn Griffith-Jones*

'The ultimate aphrodisiac' *Henry Kissinger*

'Makes **Room at the Top** look like a vicarage tea-party' *Daily Telegraph*

***See page 144**

Aphorisms and apothegms, bons
mots and bromides, epigrams and
epitaphs, repartees and rejoinders, squibs
and squelches, wise saws and wisecracks –
that is the stuff Nigel Rees' Radio 4
series 'Quote . . . Unquote' is made of.
Part quiz, part anthology, the 'Quote . . .
Unquote' book deliciously captures the
flavour of the radio series.

There are catchphrases and
spoonerisms, famous first and last words,
Sam Goldwynisms, Dorothy Parkerisms,
Margot Asquith's brilliant 'margots', and
the gaffes, goofs, immortal and mortal
remarks of Prime Ministers, Presidents,
film, radio and TV stars, and all sorts of
other people. To inspire the aspiring there
are texts for sermons. For connoisseurs of
fine food and bad English, an execrable
menu. And for those who think they know
it all, a mind-boggling array of quizzes
with a tantalising variety of scrambled
quotations and stolen titles all to
unscramble or track down.

# "Quote... Unquote"

**Nigel Rees**

**Illustrated
by
Michael ffolkes**

London
UNWIN PAPERBACKS
Boston Sydney

First published in Great Britain by
George Allen & Unwin 1978

Reprinted three times

First published in Unwin Paperbacks 1980

UNWIN ® PAPERBACKS
40 Museum Street, London WC1A 1LU

This edition © Nigel Rees 1978, 1980

Illustrations © Michael ffolkes 1978

British Library Cataloguing in Publication Data

'Quote-unquote'.
  1. Quotations, English
  I. Rees, Nigel   II. ffolkes, Michael
  808.88'2      PN6081      79–42753

  ISBN 0–04–827020–2

Paperback edition based on the
hardback designed by David Pocknell

Printed by
Cox & Wyman Ltd, Reading

# **Contents**

Nigel Rees was born near Liverpool on the day before D-Day, 1944. Since graduating with a degree in English from Oxford, he has had an extraordinarily varied career in radio and television as presenter, writer, interviewer, producer and actor. He has introduced the Radio 4 breakfast-time programme *Today*, the arts magazine *Kaleidoscope* and World Service *Twenty-Four Hours* – and has appeared in the comedy show *The Burkiss Way*. In 1976 he started the BBC Radio quiz '*Quote ... Unquote*', upon which this book is based and in 1979 *Cabbages and Kings* on ITV. He is married to the marketing director of a cosmetics firm and lives in London.

His latest books are *Graffiti Lives, OK*, a collection of the most amusing scribblings from walls all over Britain and from other corners of the globe, and *Very Interesting ... But Stupid!*, a book of catchphrases from the world of entertainment. Both are published by Unwin Paperbacks. (See page 143)

# <u>Preface</u>

This is partly a quiz-book and partly an anthology based on the BBC Radio 4 series **'Quote . . . Unquote'.**

I am inclined to interpret the word 'quote' very broadly – so you will find in these pages:

*aphorisms, apothegms, asides, banalities, barbs,* bons mots, *bromides, catchphrases, citations, clichés, commonplaces, cutting remarks, dictums, epigrams, epitaphs, mottoes, put downs, quips, quotes, references, replications, responsions, repartees, retorts, replies, rebuttals, rejoinders, ripostes, sage reflections, sayings, slogans, squelches, unquotes, unsolicited testimonials, wise saws . . . and modern instances.*

In devising the radio quiz – and now this book – I have not been restricted by considerations of comprehensiveness, durability or even usefulness, as the compiler of a dictionary of quotations might be.

The **'Quote . . . Unquote'**
book simply contains what I have
most enjoyed reading or hearing
over the past few years and have
thought worth jotting down. I hope
the overall effect for the reader will
be like opening another man's
commonplace book.

I should make plain that some
of the quotes are bogus. These are
what I call the 'unquotes' –
inventions perfectly obvious as
such, I hope. Should one ever
appear in a dictionary of quotations
I shall have to award a prize to the
person who spots it.

My thanks are due to the BBC
for putting the programme on the
air, to my estimable producer John
Lloyd for working on the idea with
me since the very beginning, and to
numerous listeners and friends for
sharing with me their favourite
quotations and pointing out
mistakes (I look forward to being
told of the ones in this book).

Those who took part in the
quiz during the first two years were
not only brave enough to have their
knowledge of quotations exposed,

they also provided much ancillary wit – some of which has found its way into this volume:

Larry Adler, Lynn Barber, Richard Boston, James Cameron, Peter Cook, Jilly Cooper, Alan Coren, Ronald Fletcher, Anna Ford, Michael Frayn, Graeme Garden, Benny Green, Germaine Greer, Irene Handl, Richard Ingrams, Jo Kendall, Roberta Leigh, Humphrey Lyttelton, Lord Mancroft, Arthur Marshall, George Melly, Jonathan Miller, Spike Milligan, Malcolm Muggeridge, Ian McKellen, Hilary Pritchard, Diana Quick, Norma Shepherd, Ned Sherrin, Miriam Stoppard, Tom Stoppard, Polly Toynbee, John Wells, Kenneth Williams, Terry Wogan.

**'They were all of them fond of quotations.'**
(Lewis Carroll, *The Hunting of the Snark*)

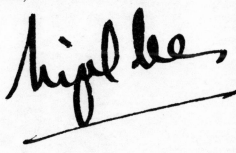

# <u>Dr Livingstone, I Presume?</u>

These notable first words were spoken by Henry Morton Stanley when at last he located the Scottish missionary and explorer near Lake Tanganyika in 1871.
Here are some more. Who said them? In what sense are they first words?

The answers are on pages 14 and 15.

## 1
Mr Watson, come here, I want to see you.

## 2
We knocked the bastard off.

## 3
That's one small step for man, one giant leap for mankind.

## 4
Tennis, anyone?

## 5
You ain't heard nothin' yet.

**6**

God be glorified.

**7**

The past is a foreign country: they do things differently there.

**8**

As I was saying when I was interrupted, it is a powerful hard thing to please all the people all the time.

# **Answers**
## Dr Livingstone, I Presume?

### 1

The first words spoken over the telephone by its inventor, Alexander Graham Bell, March 1876.

### 2

Edmund Hillary on being the first to reach the summit of Mount Everest, May 1953. cf. George Leigh Mallory's reply when asked why he wanted to do the same: 'Because it's there.'

### 3

The first words spoken on the moon by Neil Armstrong, July 1969.

### 4

Humphrey Bogart's sole line in his first stage appearance.

### 5

Ad lib remark by Al Jolson in *The Jazz Singer*, the first full-length talking picture, released in New York, October 1927.

## 6

Reputed to be the first words of St Nicholas as he leapt from his mother's womb – as in Benjamin Britten's cantata *St Nicholas*.

## 7

The opening words of L. P. Hartley's novel *The Go-Between*.

## 8

William Connor, 'Cassandra' of the *Daily Mirror*, resuming his column after the war, September 1946 and echoing words attributed to Abraham Lincoln – 'You can fool all the people some of the time, and some of the people all the time, but you can't fool all the people all of the time.'

# <u>Oh, Bitchery!</u>

'You should learn not to make personal remarks,' said Alice to the Mad Hatter – but it did not stop him and it has not stopped anyone else from doing so.
Here is a selection of my favourite personal remarks, ranging from the mildly censorious to the ambiguously flattering:

He didn't need to take a change of shoes. He can always wear hers. She has very big feet, you know.

> *Vivien Merchant, Harold Pinter's wife, when he left her for Lady Antonia Fraser.*

He rose without trace.

> *Kitty Muggeridge on David Frost.*

No more coals to Newcastle, no more Hoares to Paris.

> *King George V made this remark when Sir Samuel Hoare, the Foreign Secretary, concluded the Hoare-Laval pact (which virtually consigned Abyssinia to the Italians) in Paris.*

Winston has devoted the best years of his life to preparing his impromptu speeches.

> *F. E. Smith.*

He is a self-made man and worships his creator.

*John Bright on Disraeli.*

The only thing I really mind about going to prison is the thought of Lord Longford coming to visit me.

*Richard Ingrams, editor of* Private Eye.

Too clever by three-quarters.

*said of Jonathan Miller.*

Dame Edith Evans was told that Nancy Mitford had been lent a villa so that she could finish a book: 'Oh really. What exactly is she reading?'

Reminds me of nothing so much as a dead fish before it has had time to stiffen.

> *George Orwell's remark about Clement Attlee typifies the inordinate amount of personal abuse Attlee had levelled at him. Churchill is said to have called him 'a sheep in sheep's clothing' and 'a modest little man with much to be modest about'. A popular saying was, 'An empty taxi drew up and out got Clem Attlee.'*

In defeat unbeatable, in victory unbearable.

> *Churchill on Montgomery.*

A legend in his own lunchtime.

> *Christopher Wordsworth, literary critic, on Clifford Makins, sporting journalist.*

That woman speaks eighteen languages, and she can't say 'no' in any of them.

*Dorothy Parker*.

He looks like the guy in a science fiction movie who is the first to see the Creature.

> *David Frye's description of President Gerald R. Ford is one of many.*

Others are:

He played too much football without a helmet.

He can't eat gum and walk at the same time.

He'd fuck up a two-car funeral.

_____

She could eat an apple through a tennis racquet.

> *Said of a toothy character in Noel Coward's* Come into the Garden, Maud.

Two of the nicest people if ever there was one.

> *Alan Bennett on Sidney and Beatrice Webb.*

_____

**Randolph Churchill went into hospital to have a lung removed and it was announced that the trouble was not malignant.
Evelyn Waugh commented:**

**'A typical triumph of modern science to find the only part of Randolph that was not malignant and remove it.'**

What the proprietorship of these papers is aiming at is power, and power without responsibility, the prerogative of the harlot throughout the ages.

*Harold Macmillan was present at the by-election meeting in 1931 when Baldwin made this attack on the Press Barons. He recalls his father-in-law, the Duke of Devonshire, commenting: 'Good God, that's done it. He's lost us the tarts' vote.'*

# The 'T' Is Silent

In any digest of personal remarks Margot Asquith,
wife of the Liberal Prime Minister,
deserves a section to herself.
Sometimes she dropped bricks and was downright
insulting, on other occasions she produced wonderful
*margots*, vivid verbal snapshots like these:

He could not see a belt without hitting below it.

*of Lloyd George.*

My dear old friend King George V always told me
that he would never have died but for that vile
doctor.

*of Lord Dawson of Penn.*

His modesty amounts to deformity.

*of her husband.*

She tells enough white lies to ice a cake.

*of a female acquaintance.*

He has a brilliant mind until he makes it up.

*of Sir Stafford Cripps.*

I saw him riding in the Row, clinging to his horse like a string of onions.

*of Lord Hugh Cecil.*

An imitation rough diamond.

*of a US General.*

She's as tough as an ox. She'll be turned into Bovril when she dies.

*of a friend.*

Very clever, but his brains go to his head.

*of F. E. Smith.*

On a visit to Hollywood,
Margot Asquith met Jean Harlow.
Apparently, the film-star had not encountered
the name 'Margot' before
and asked if the 't' was pronounced or not.
Came the reply:

'No. The "t" is silent – as in Harlow.'

He had one arm round your waist and one eye on the clock.

*of a politician.*

# <u>Kinquering Congs</u>
# <u>Their Titles Take</u> – 1

Pity poor Peter Scott, the naturalist, when he came to choose the title for his autobiography. He set his heart on *The Eye of the Wind* but nowhere could he find a poem or piece of suitable prose containing the phrase. Eventually, in desperation, he asked C. Day Lewis to write a poem from which he could quote it.
The following writers of bibliography or autobiography did not have to go to such desperate lengths for their titles.

Where did they go?
The answers are on pages 30 to 32.

**1**
Hugh Cudlipp: **Publish and be Damned.**

**2**
Sir Francis Chichester: **The Lonely Sea and the Sky.**

**3**
Dennis Wheatley: **The Time has come the Young Man said.**

**4**

Lilli Palmer: **Change Lobsters and Dance.**

**5**

T. E. Lawrence: **Seven Pillars of Wisdom.**

**6**

Richard Hillary: **The Last Enemy.**

**7**

Duff Cooper: **Old Men Forget.**

**8**

The Duchess of Windsor: **The Heart has its Reasons.**

**9**

Hugh Dalton: **Call Back Yesterday.**

**10**

Lord George-Brown: **In My Way.**

'Old men forget'

Where did these writers and composers of plays and musicals find their titles?

## 11
Thornton Wilder: **The Skin of our Teeth.**

## 12
J. M. Barrie: **Dear Brutus.**

## 13
George Bernard Shaw: **Arms and the Man.**

## 14
Noel Coward: **Sigh No More.**

## 15
Noel Coward: **This Happy Breed.**

## 16
Noel Coward: **Blithe Spirit.**

## 17
Ivor Novello: **Perchance to Dream.**

## 18
Dorothy Reynolds and Julian Slade: **Salad Days.**

## 19
Kenneth Tynan and Co.: **Oh, Calcutta.**

# **Answers**
## Kinquering Congs
## Their Titles Take – 1

**1** The Duke of Wellington's response when a former mistress threatened to publish her diary and letters.

**2** John Masefield's poem *Sea Fever*.

**3** ' "The time has come," the Walrus said, / "To talk of many things" ' (Carroll, *Through the Looking-Glass*) coupled with ' "You are old," Father William," the Young Man said' (Carroll, *Alice's Adventures in Wonderland*).

**4** Also a reference to *Alice's Adventures in Wonderland*, though these precise words do not appear in 'The Lobster Quadrille'.

**5** 'Wisdom hath builded her house, she hath hewn out her seven pillars' – Proverbs ix.1.

**6** 'The last enemy that shall be destroyed is death' – 1 Corinthians xv.26.

**7** 'Old men forget . . . / But he'll remember with advantages / What feats he did that day [St Crispin's Day]' – Shakespeare, *Henry V*, IV.iii.

**8** 'Le cœur a ses raisons que la raison ne connaît point' – Pascal, *Pensées*.

**9** 'O! call back yesterday, bid time return' – Shakespeare, *Richard II*, III.ii.

**10** Lord George-Brown attributes it to 'My Way' though the song does not include this phrase.

**11** 'I am escaped with the skin of my teeth' – Job xix.20.

**12** 'The fault, dear Brutus, is not in our stars' – Shakespeare, *Julius Caesar*, I.ii.

**13** 'Arma virumque cano' – the opening words of Virgil's *Aeneid*, or from Dryden's translation: 'Arms, and the man I sing.'

**14** 'Sigh no more, ladies, sigh no more / Men were deceivers ever' – Shakespeare, *Much Ado about Nothing*, I.iii.

**15** 'This Royal throne of kings, this sceptr'd isle / . . . this happy breed of men' – Shakespeare, *Richard II*, II.i.

**16** 'Hail to thee, blithe spirit, bird thou never wert' – Shelley, 'To a Skylark'.

**17** 'To die, to sleep: / To sleep, perchance to dream' – Shakespeare, *Hamlet*, III.i.

**18** 'My salad days, when I was green in judgement, cold in blood' – Shakespeare, *Antony and Cleopatra*, I.v.

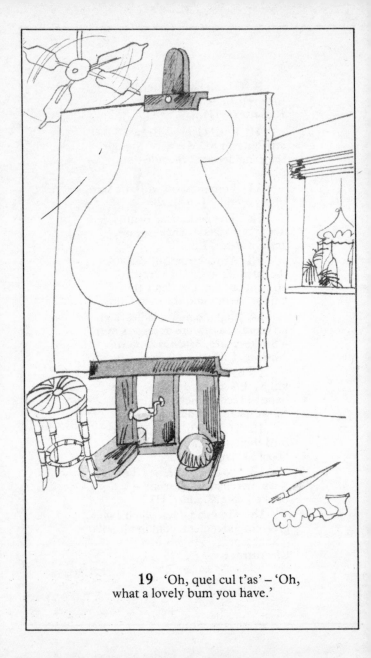

**19** 'Oh, quel cul t'as' – 'Oh, what a lovely bum you have.'

# Like The Curate's Egg – 1

The Du Maurier cartoon 'True Humility' appeared in *Punch* on 19 November 1895. It showed a bishop at breakfast with a curate, and the caption read:

**Rt Rev. Host**
I'm afraid you've got a bad egg, Mr Jones.
**The Curate**
Oh no, my Lord, I assure you! Parts of it are excellent.

Like the Curate's egg, the following quotations are good in parts, but parts of them are scrambled. What was the original quotation? What is the source?

The answers are on pages 36 and 37.

**1**
There is a tide in the affairs of women which, taken at the flood, leads – God knows where.

## 2

A rose-red city, half as Golders Green.

## 3

Vasectomy means not ever having to say you're sorry.

## 4

Brevity is the soul of lingerie.

## 5

'Tis better to have loved and lost than never to have lost at all.

## 6

Man is born free but everywhere is in cellular underwear.

## 7

Kinquering congs their titles take.

## 8

Where there is no television, the people perish.

## 9

Live music is an anachronism, and now is the winter of our discothèque.

## 10

I awoke one morning and found myself famished.

## 11

Oh, wad some power the giftie gie us to see some people before they see us.

**12**

Ralph Reader, I married him.

**13**

When I am dead and opened, you shall find 'Callous' engraved upon my heart.

**14**

Great oafs from little infants grow.

# **Answers**

## <u>Like The Curate's Egg – 1</u>

**1** 'There is a tide in the affairs of men,/Which, taken at the flood, leads on to fortune' – Shakespeare, *Julius Caesar*, IV.iii. (Scrambled by Byron in *Don Juan*.)

**2** 'A rose-red city – "half as old as time"!' – Rev. John William Burgon, *Petra*. The quote-within-a-quote refers to 'By many a temple half as old as time', from *Italy: a farewell* by Samuel Rogers. (Scrambled by Muir and Norden in their sketch *Balham: Gateway to the South*, performed on record by Peter Sellers.)

**3** 'Love means not ever having to say you're sorry' – Erich Segal, *Love Story*. (Scrambled by Larry Adler who once took part in an edition of *Quote . . . Unquote* on his way to have a vasectomy.)

**4** 'Brevity is the soul of wit' – the proverb, which makes its first recorded appearance in Shakespeare's *Hamlet*, II.ii. (Scrambled by Dorothy Parker.)

**5** ''Tis better to have loved and lost / Than never to have loved at all' – Tennyson, *In Memoriam*. (Scrambled by Samuel Butler in *Erewhon*.)

**6** 'Man was born free and everywhere he is in chains' – Jean-Jacques Rousseau, *Du Contrat Social*. (Scrambled by Jonathan Miller in *Beyond the Fringe*.)

**7** 'Conquering Kings their titles take' – from the hymn by John Chandler. (Scrambled by Rev. W. A. Spooner, supposedly when announcing the hymn in New College chapel, Oxford. As it was not the custom to announce hymns in his day this is one of many 'spoonerisms' of doubtful authenticity.)

**8** 'Where there is no vision, the people perish' – Proverbs xxix.18.

**9** 'Now is the winter of our discontent' – Shakespeare, *Richard III*, I.i. (Scrambled by Benny Green in a newspaper article.)

**10** 'I awoke one morning and found myself famous' – Byron on the instantaneous success of *Childe Harold*.

**11** 'O wad some Pow'r the giftie gie us / To see oursels as others see us' – Robert Burns, *To a louse*. (Scrambled by Ethel Watts Mumford.)

**12** 'Reader, I married him' – the opening words of the last chapter of *Jane Eyre* by Charlotte Brontë, referring to Mr Rochester rather than the founder of the Boy Scout *Gang Show*.

**13** 'When I am dead and opened you shall find "Calais" lying in my heart' – the saying attributed to Mary Tudor, Calais having been lost to the French after two hundred years as an English possession. (Scrambled by Sellars and Yeatman in *1066 and all that*.)

**14** 'Great oaks from little acorns grow' – the proverb. (Scrambled by various people. Another version, concerning Nikita Kruschev, is 'Great oafs from little ikons grow.')

# Cheer Up, The *Wurst* Is Yet To Come

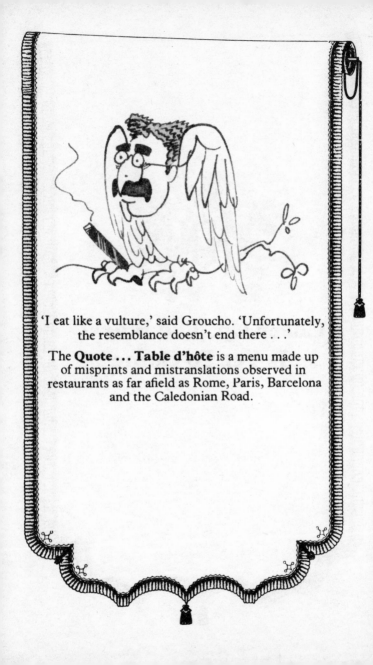

'I eat like a vulture,' said Groucho. 'Unfortunately, the resemblance doesn't end there . . .'

The **Quote . . . Table d'hôte** is a menu made up of misprints and mistranslations observed in restaurants as far afield as Rome, Paris, Barcelona and the Caledonian Road.

Half fresh grapefruit
Satiated calamary
Hen soup
Hard egg with sauce mayonnaise
Frightened eggs

Dreaded veal cutlet
Larks in the spit
Spited rooster
Battered codpieces
A kind of long
Utmost of chicken
Veal Gordon Blue
Raped carrots

Sweet smalls pie★
Tarts of the house at pleasure

Café au lit

★ 'Age cannot wither it, nor custard stale
its infinite variety' Shakespeare,
*Antony and Cleopatra* I.ii.

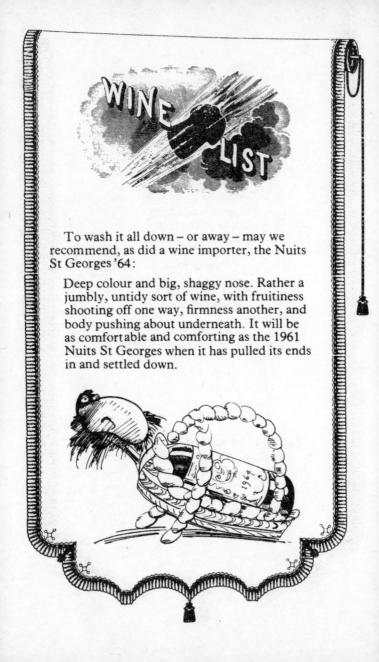

To wash it all down – or away – may we
recommend, as did a wine importer, the Nuits
St Georges '64:

Deep colour and big, shaggy nose. Rather a
jumbly, untidy sort of wine, with fruitiness
shooting off one way, firmness another, and
body pushing about underneath. It will be
as comfortable and comforting as the 1961
Nuits St Georges when it has pulled its ends
in and settled down.

To round off the meal, a drop of port perhaps? Lord Mancroft remembers how Stephen Potter, inventor of One-Upmanship, once promoted a Cockburn '97 which was clearly past its best. He spoke of:

the imperial decay of the invalid port . . . its gracious withdrawal from perfection . . . keeping a hint of former majesty, withal . . . whilst it hovered between oblivion and the divine *Untergang* of infinite recession.

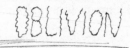

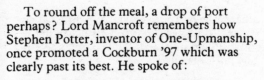

# **Replies Retorts Ripostes**

Lord Nuffield, the motor magnate, had dined at an Oxford college. A porter produced his hat rather briskly and Nuffield inquired, 'How d'you know it's mine?' The porter replied:

> *I don't, my Lord. But it's the one you came with.*

Martin Routh (1755–1854) was President of Magdalen College, Oxford, and a man of great composure – so much so that when an excitable Fellow rushed up to announce that a member of the college had killed himself, Routh replied:

> *Pray, don't tell me who. Allow me to guess.*

Sir Thomas Beecham was travelling in the no-smoking carriage of a train when a woman passenger lit a cigarette with the words, 'You won't object if I smoke?' To which Beecham replied, 'Certainly not – and you won't object if I'm sick.'
It was in the days when the railways were still privately owned. 'I don't think you know who I am,' the woman angrily pointed out. 'I am one of the directors' wives.' To which Beecham riposted:

> *Madam, if you were the director's only wife, I should still be sick.*

When Samuel Goldwyn asked Bernard Shaw if he could buy the film rights to his plays, G.B.S. declined the offer thus:

> *The trouble is, Mr Goldwyn, that you are only interested in art and I am only interested in money.*

Horatio Bottomley, the Independent MP sent to gaol for fraudulent conversion in 1922, was discovered sewing mail-bags by a prison visitor. 'Ah, Bottomley,' he remarked. 'Sewing?'

> *No, reaping.*

Eva Perón once visited Europe but was not received as she thought appropriate for the powerful wife of the ruler of Argentina. She failed to get an invitation to tea at Buckingham Palace or the Papal honour she hoped for in Rome. And in northern Italy she complained to her host that a voice in a crowd had called her a 'whore'. He replied:

> *Quite so. But I have not been on a ship for fifteen years and they still call me 'Admiral'.*

It was suggested to Tennyson that the marriage of Thomas and Jane Carlyle was a mistake. With anyone but each other they might have been perfectly happy:

> *I totally disagree with you. By any other arrangement four people would have been unhappy instead of two.*

'Pearls before swine'

Calvin Coolidge once made a notable squelch. A young girl gushed: 'Oh, Mr President, Poppa says that if I can get three words out of you he will buy me a fur coat.'

*Poppa wins.*

Dorothy Parker, when told that Coolidge was dead, remarked:

*How can they tell?*

And, although said to be apocryphal, there is the story of Dorothy Parker going through a swing-door with Clare Boothe Luce who said – as one does on such occasions – 'Age before beauty.' Going ahead first, Parker said:

*Pearls before swine.*

Mandy Rice-Davies, one of the call-girls in the Profumo Affair, 1963, appeared at a magistrates' hearing. She was asked if she was aware that the then Lord Astor had denied her statement that she had been to bed with him:

*Well, he would, wouldn't he?*

F. E. Smith, Earl of Birkenhead, taunted Lord Chief Justice Hewart about the size of his stomach. 'What's it to be – a boy or a girl?'

> *If it's a boy I'll call him John. If it's a girl I'll call her Mary. But if, as I suspect, it's only wind, I'll call it F. E. Smith.*

The Irish actor-manager Anew McMaster was travelling with his company by train one Sunday when it stopped at an isolated rural station. Lowering the window and revealing his extravagant hat and other thespian garb, McMaster inquired of a porter, 'What country, friend, is this?' Being an educated Irish railway employee, the porter recognised Viola's opening lines from *Twelfth Night* and promptly gave Shakespeare's own reply:

> *This is Illyria – lady.*

Jack Benny, to the robber who demanded 'Your money or your life!':

> *I'm thinking it over.*

W. C. Fields, when asked whether he liked children:

> *Boiled or fried?*

Shaw sent Churchill two tickets for the first night of *St Joan*, 'one for yourself, one for a friend – if you have one'. Expressing regret at not being able to attend, Churchill replied by requesting tickets for the second night:

> *If there is one.*

Towards the end of his life, Churchill was sitting in the House of Commons smoking room with his fly-buttons undone. When this was pointed out to him, he said:

> *Dead birds don't fall out of nests.*

A business-like exchange of notes in the eighteenth century between the Prince de Joinville and the actress, Mlle Rachel. He asked, 'Where? When? How much?' She answered:

> *Your place. Tonight. Free.*

Groucho Marx was going down in the lift at the Hotel Danieli in Venice. At the fourth floor a group of priests got in. One of them recognised Groucho and said, 'Excuse me, Mr Marx, but my mother was a great fan of yours.' To which Groucho retorted:

> *I didn't know you guys were allowed to have mothers.*

The wife of Chico Marx caught him kissing a chorus-girl. A row ensued, tempers flared, but the only explanation Chico offered was:

> *I wasn't kissing her. I was whispering in her mouth.*

A fan accosted James Joyce in Zurich with the words 'May I kiss the hand that wrote *Ulysses*?' Joyce refused saying:

> *No, it did a lot of other things, too.*

In the First World War, Lytton Strachey appeared before a military tribunal to put his case as a conscientious objector. He was asked by the chairman what he would do if he saw a German soldier trying to rape his sister:

> *I would try to get between them.*

When Ringo Starr was asked what was the greatest threat to the Beatles – the H-Bomb or dandruff, he answered:

> *The H-Bomb. We've already got dandruff.*

When Noel Coward was confronted by middle-aged female fans who began, 'Oh, Mr Coward, you don't know me . . .', he would say:

> *But, of course, I do. And how is Mabel?*

Coward watched the Coronation on TV in New York. When the carriage bearing Queen Salote of Tonga came into view a friend asked, 'Who's the fellow sitting with her?' In fact, it was the Sultan of Kelantan but Coward suggested:

> *Her lunch.*

# There's No Answer To That

**Frank Finlay (as Casanova)**
I'll be perfectly frank with you – I have a long felt want.
**Eric Morecambe**
There's no answer to that.

Here are some more remarks to which a reply is neither recorded nor, in most cases, conceivable:

Which of us has not felt in his heart a half-warmed fish?

*Rev. W. A. Spooner.*

Tell me, was it you or your brother who was killed in the war?

*Spooner, again.*

Anyone who isn't confused here doesn't really understand what's going on.

*Belfast citizen, 1970.*

Ah well, they say it's not as bad as they say it is.

*Southern Irish woman on the situation in Ulster.*

A great man! Why, I doubt if there are six his equal in the whole of Boston.

> *Unnamed Bostonian to Gladstone about Shakespeare.*

The most delightful advantage of being bald – one can *hear* snowflakes.

> *R. G. Daniels.*

Ernie Byfield Jnr, son of the American hotel owner, was asked why he – such a young man – was running three big hotels:

> *Well, I happened to run into my father in the lobby and he took a liking to me.*

Oh no, thank you, I only smoke on special occasions.

> *Labour minister when asked if he would like a cigar, while dining with King George VI.*

The down trains will be delayed owing to the late arrival of the up trains.

> *Station announcer at Waterloo.*

Welsh miner, when asked if he was ready to strike, in 1973:

> *We have girded up our loins and tied up the loose ends.*

A woman without a man is like a fish without a bicycle.

> *Graffito at Birmingham University (and elsewhere).*

Why did He not marry? Could the answer be that Jesus was not by nature the marrying sort?

> *Hugh Montefiore, when Vicar of St Mary's, Cambridge.*

I used to be indecisive, but now I'm not so sure.

> *Boscoe Pertwee (eighteenth-century wit).*

The soil is fertile, sir, because it is full of micro-orgasms.

> *Thirteen-year-old pupil at Cranleigh.*

When Sir John Gielgud told a theatrical company that all the men must wear jock-straps under their leotards, a voice piped up:

> *Please, Sir John, does that apply to those of us who only have small parts?*

I wouldn't believe Hitler was dead, even if he told me so himself.

> *Hjalmar Schacht, Hitler's Central Bank Governor, 8 May 1945.*

I think that the gentleman who created 'King Kong' would have been more gainfully employed in making a set of concrete steps at the Ashton Road end of Bracebridge Street to help old people get to the bus without having to make half-mile detours.

> *Letter to the* Birmingham Evening Mail, *May 1972.*

Is it a book that you would have lying around in your own house? Is this a book that you would even wish your wife or your servant to read?

> *Mervyn Griffith-Jones, prosecuting counsel at the* Lady Chatterley *trial, 1961.*

The weather will be cold. There are two reasons for this. One is that the temperatures will be lower.

> *Radio weather forecast, 12 April 1969.*

You should make a point of trying every experience once – except incest and folk dancing.

> *Scotsman (quoted by Arnold Bax).*

# Quote ... Misquote

Misquotation is not necessarily a vice. We tend to rearrange words to make them easier to utter. We may attribute words to a speaker which he did not actually say but which convey the spirit of what he said.
In what way are these misquotes? What was originally said or meant?

The answers are on pages 60 to 62.

**1**

I knew him well, Horatio.

**2**

Play it again, Sam.

**3**

Thou shalt not kill / But needst not strive officiously to keep alive.

**4**

We are the masters now.

**5**

All that glitters is not gold.

**6**

Come up and see me some time.

**7**

Lead on, Macduff.

**8**

I want to be alone.

**9**
First catch your hare.

**10**
Survival of the fittest.

**11**
Pride goeth before a fall.

**12**
The stuff that dreams are made of.

**13**
Money is the root of all evil.

**14**
Elementary, my dear Watson.

**15**
I must go down to the seas again.

**16**
To gild the lily.

**17**
You dirty rat.

# **Answers**
## Quote . . . Misquote

### 1

Hamlet's actual words are: 'Alas! poor Yorick. I knew him, Horatio' – (*Hamlet*, V.i)

### 2

Nowhere in the film *Casablanca* does Humphrey Bogart say this phrase. At one point Ingrid Bergman says, 'Play it once, Sam, for old time's sake' and later on Bogart says, 'You played it for her, you can play it for me. Play it.'

### 3

Arthur Hugh Clough's *The Latest Decalogue* was an *ironical* version of the Ten Commandments – not serious advice to doctors (in which sense it is often quoted now).

### 4

What Sir Hartley Shawcross said in the House of Commons in April 1946 was: 'We [Labour] are the masters *at the moment* – and not only for the moment but for a very long time to come.'

### 5

If quoting from *The Merchant of Venice* (II.vii): 'All that *glisters* is not gold.'

## 6

Nowhere in the film *She done him wrong* does Mae West say the words in that order. She says: 'You know I always did like a man in uniform. And that one fits you grand. Why don't you *come up some time and see me.*'

## 7

'*Lay on*, Macduff. / And damn'd be him that first cries, "Hold enough!"'' – *Macbeth*, V.vii.

## 8

'I never said I want to be alone,' Garbo once remarked. 'I only said I want to be *let* alone.' Indeed, no one has been able to find mention of the famous phrase in any newspaper reports of her early days in Hollywood. After it had caught on, however, she herself used it in various films.

## 9

A misquote and usually misattributed, too. Not Mrs Beeton but Mrs Hannah Glasse wrote 'Take your hare when it is cased' in *The Art of Cookery made plain and easy*, 1747.

## 10

Herbert Spencer meant the survival of the most suitable, not of the most fit physically.

## 11

'*Pride goeth before destruction* and an haughty spirit before a fall' – Proverbs xvi.18.

## 12

'We are such stuff / As dreams are made *on*' – *The Tempest*.

## 13

'*The love of money* is the root of all evil' – 1 Timothy vi.10.

## 14

The nearest the great detective gets to saying this occurs in *The Memoirs of Sherlock Holmes* when he remarks to Watson: 'Elementary.'

## 15

'I must down to the seas again' – Masefield, *Sea Fever*.

## 16

In quoting *King John* (IV.ii): '*To gild refined gold*, to paint the lily.'

## 17

James Cagney claims he never said the words put in his mouth by numerous impressionists. In *Blonde Crazy*, however, he calls someone a 'dirty, double-crossing rat'.

# A Week Is A Long Time in Politics

Uncharacteristically, Sir Harold Wilson says he is unable to remember when he first uttered what is without doubt the most quoted political remark of recent years – 'A week is a long time in politics'.

What is more, he says 'it does not mean I'm living from day to day', but was intended as 'a prescription for long-term strategic thinking and planning, ignoring the day-to-day issues and pressures which may hit the headlines but which must not be allowed to get out of focus while longer-term policies are taking effect'.

It seems most probable that in its present form the phrase was first uttered at a meeting of the Parliamentary Lobby in the wake of the Sterling crisis shortly after Harold Wilson came to power in 1964.

However, Robert Carvel of the London *Evening Standard* recalls Wilson at a Labour Party conference in 1960 saying 'Forty-eight hours is a long time in politics'.

Even quotes are prone to inflation.

Some more political sayings from the past decade or two are recalled in the next few pages. See also the chapters *Expletive Deleted* and *Better Left Unsaid*.

I thought the best thing to do was to settle up these *little local difficulties* and then return to the wider vision of the Commonwealth.

> *Harold Macmillan said this on leaving for the Commonwealth Conference in 1958. Peter Thorneycroft, his Chancellor of the Exchequer, and two Treasury ministers had just resigned.*

Every time Mr Macmillan comes back from abroad Mr Butler goes to the airport and grips him warmly by the throat.

> *Harold Wilson.*

Greater love hath no man than this, that he lay down his friends for his life.

> *Jeremy Thorpe, on Harold Macmillan's 'Night of the Long Knives' when he sacked half his Cabinet, 1962.*

I think the Prime Minister has to be a butcher and know the joints. That is perhaps where I have not been competent enough in knowing the ways that you cut up a carcass.

> *R. A. Butler (cf. Gladstone: 'The first essential for a Prime Minister is to be a good butcher.')*

I am on the right wing of the middle of the road
with a strong radical bias.

> *Anthony Wedgwood-Benn in the*
> *mid-1950s.*

If the British public falls for Labour's policies, I say
it will be stark staring bonkers.

> *Quintin Hogg, before the 1964 general*
> *election which brought Labour to*
> *power.*

Most British statesmen have either drunk too much
or womanised too much. I never fell into the second
category.

> *Lord George-Brown.*

Lord George-Brown drunk is a better man than the
Prime Minister sober.

> *Leader in* The Times.

I'm an optimist. But I'm an optimist who takes his
raincoat.

> *Harold Wilson.*

It is the unacceptable face of capitalism but one
should not suggest that the whole of British in-
dustry consists of practices of this kind.

> *Edward Heath on the Lonrho Affair,*
> *1973.*

As I look ahead I am filled with foreboding. Like the Roman I seem to see 'The River Tiber foaming with much blood'.

> *Enoch Powell's audience in Birmingham, April 1968, immediately spotted this as a reference to Virgil's* Aeneid, Book Six: '*Et Thybrim multo spumantem sanguine cerno.*'

All political lives, unless they are cut off in midstream at a happy juncture, end in failure, because that is the nature of politics and of human affairs.

> *Enoch Powell.*

Bunnies *can* (and *will*) go to France.

> *Jeremy Thorpe to a Mr Norman Scott, 1961.*

Ich bin ein Berliner.

> *President Kennedy, West Berlin, 1963. (According to Ben Bradlee he spent 'the better part of an hour' learning how to pronounce this phrase.)*

I would remind you that extremism in the defense of liberty is no vice and . . . that moderation in the pursuit of justice is no virtue.

> *Senator Barry Goldwater, 1964.*

The Prime Minister is stealing our clothes . . . but he's going to look pretty ridiculous walking around in mine.

*Margaret Thatcher, 1977.*

We have, of course, often done it before, but never on a pavement outside a hotel in Eastbourne. We have done it in various rooms in one way or another at various functions. It is perfectly genuine and normal – and normal and right – so to do.

*William Whitelaw on kissing Margaret Thatcher, 1975.*

All reactionaries are paper tigers.

*Mao Tse-Tung.*

You won the election. But I won the count.

*Anastasio Somoza, Nicaraguan dictator.*

Power is the ultimate aphrodisiac.*

*Henry Kissinger.*

*This should not be confused with Lord Acton's dictum: 'All power tends to be an aphrodisiac and absolute power leaves you feeling rotten by Wednesday.'

# <u>Kinquering Congs</u><br><u>Their Titles Take – 2</u>

Where did these kinquering novelists take their titles from?

The answers are on pages 74 to 76.

**1**
William Thackeray: **Vanity Fair.**

**2**
Frederick Forsyth: **The Dogs of War.**

**3**
John Steinbeck: **The Grapes of Wrath.**

**4**
John Steinbeck: **Of Mice and Men.**

**5**
Ernest Hemingway: **For Whom the Bell Tolls.**

**6**
Nigel Balchin: **Mine Own Executioner.**

**7**
James Jones: **From here to Eternity.**

**8**

W. Somerset Maugham: **Cakes and Ale.**

**9**

Mary Webb: **Precious Bane.**

**10**

Taylor Caldwell: **Captains and the Kings.**

**11**

Aldous Huxley: **Antic Hay.**

**12**

Aldous Huxley: **Brave New World.**

**13**

Susan Howatch: **The Rich are Different.**

**14**

Simon Raven: the **Alms for Oblivion** series.

**15**

Thomas Hardy: **Under the Greenwood Tree.**

**16**

Angus Wilson: **Anglo-Saxon Attitudes.**

**17**

Thomas Hardy: **Far from the Madding Crowd.**

**18**

H. E. Bates: **The Darling Buds of May.**

**19**

T. H. White: **The Once and Future King.**

**20**

Malcolm Bradbury: **Eating People is Wrong.**

# **Answers**
## Kinquering Congs
## Their Titles Take – 2

**1**

'It beareth the name of Vanity-Fair, because the town where 'tis kept, is lighter than vanity' – Bunyan, *Pilgrim's Progress.*

**2**

'Cry "Havoc!" and let slip the dogs of war' – Shakespeare, *Julius Caesar*, III.i.

**3**

'Mine eyes have seen the glory of the coming of the Lord : / He is trampling out the vintage where the grapes of wrath are stored' – Julia Ward Howe, *The Battle Hymn of the Republic.*

**4**

'The best laid schemes o' mice an' men / Gang aft a-gley' – Robert Burns, *To a Mouse.*

**5**

'Any man's death diminishes me, because I am involved in Mankind ; And therefore never send to know for whom the bell tolls ; It tolls for thee' – John Donne, *Devotions.*

## 6

'But I do nothing upon my self, and yet I am mine own
Executioner' – John Donne, *Devotions* (again).

## 7

'Gentlemen-rankers out on the spree, / Damned from here
Eternity' – Rudyard Kipling, *Gentlemen Rankers*.

## 8

'Dost thou think, because thou art virtuous, there shall
be no more cakes and ale?' – Shakespeare,
*Twelfth Night*, II.iii.

## 9

'Let none admire / That riches grow in hell; that soil may
best / Deserve the precious bane' – Milton, *Paradise Lost*.

## 10

'The tumult and the shouting dies; / The Captains and
the Kings depart' – Kipling, *Recessional*.

## 11

'My men, like satyrs grazing on the lawns, / Shall with
their goat-feet dance an antic hay' – Marlowe, *Edward II*.

## 12

'O brave new world, / That has such people in't' –
Shakespeare, *The Tempest*, V.i.

## 13

F. Scott Fitzgerald: 'The rich are different from us.'
Ernest Hemingway: 'Yes, they have more money.'

## 14

'Time hath, my lord, a wallet at his back, / Wherein he
puts alms for oblivion' – Shakespeare,
*Troilus and Cressida*, III.iii.

## 15

'Under the greenwood tree / Who loves to lie with me' –
Shakespeare, *As You Like It*, II.v.

## 16

'He's an Anglo-Saxon Messenger – and those are Anglo-
Saxon attitudes' – Carroll, *Through the Looking-Glass*.

## 17

'Far from the madding crowd's ignoble strife' –
Gray, *Elegy Written in a Country Churchyard*.

## 18

'Rough winds do shake the darling buds of May' –
Shakespeare, *Sonnets*, 18.

## 19

'Hic jacet Arthurus, rex quondam, rexque futurus' –
Malory, *Le'Morte d'Arthur*.

## 20

Song, *The Reluctant Cannibal*, by Flanders and Swann.

# <u>Let's Fill the Whole Screen With Tits</u>

Hunt Stromberg, the American film producer, was discussing a documentary about the South Seas. 'Boys, I've got an idea,' he declared. 'Let's fill the whole screen with tits.'

Joseph von Sternberg, the director, said of Hollywood:

> *You can seduce a man's wife there, attack his daughter and wipe your hands on his canary, but if you don't like his movie, you're dead.*

When Norma Shearer, the actress, and Irving Thalberg, the producer, had their first baby, Eddie Cantor sent them a telegram:

CONGRATULATIONS ON YOUR LATEST PRODUCTION STOP SURE IT WILL LOOK BETTER AFTER IT HAS BEEN CUT STOP

Alfred Hitchcock was once reported as saying that 'Actors are like cattle.' But he denied this.

*What I said was 'Actors should be treated like cattle.'*

*Now, try your hand at spotting who said these famous lines and in which films.*

*The answers are on pages 80 and 82.*

**1**

In a month from now this Hollywood big shot's going to give you what you want.

Too late. They start shooting in a week.

I'm going to make him an offer he can't refuse.

## 2

Fasten your seat-belts. It's gonna be a bumpy night.

## 3

You know what the fellow said . . . in Italy for thirty years under the Borgias they had warfare, terror, murder, bloodshed but they produced Michelangelo, Leonardo da Vinci, and the Renaissance. In Switzerland, they had brotherly love, they had five hundred years of democracy and peace. And what did that produce? The cuckoo-clock.

## 4

Water? Do I need it. I've had to shoot my horse.

## 5

You know you don't have to act with me, Steve. You don't have to say anything, and you don't have to do anything. Not a thing . . . or maybe just whistle. You know how to whistle, don't you, Steve? You just put your lips together and blow.

## 6

Louis, I think this is the beginning of a beautiful friendship.

## 7

Tomorrow is another day.

## 8

I think it would be fun to run a newspaper.

## 9

Nobody's perfect!

## 10

Beulah, peel me a grape.

# **Answers**
## Let's Fill The Whole Screen With Tits

**1**

Marlon Brando, *The Godfather*.

**2**

Bette Davis, *All About Eve*.

**3**

Orson Welles, *The Third Man*. (In fact, he added these lines to the Graham Greene-Carol Reed script.)

**4**

Clark Gable in a B picture, *The Painted Desert* – his first words on screen.

**5**

Lauren Bacall to Humphrey Bogart, *To Have and Have Not*.

'Water? Do I need it. I've had to shoot my horse.'

## 6

Humphrey Bogart to Claude Rains, the last words of
*Casablanca*.

## 7

Vivien Leigh, *Gone With the Wind* –last words (also of
Margaret Mitchell's book).

## 8

The last words of *Citizen Kane*. Kane's last word is, of
course, 'Rosebud'.

## 9

Joe E. Brown to Jack Lemmon, the last words of
*Some Like it Hot*.

## 10

Mae West, *I'm No Angel*.

# **Samuel Goldfish Productions**

When a Pole arrived in the United States bearing an unpronounceable monicker, an immigration official renamed him 'Goldfish'. Eventually he realised the trick that had been played on him and took the name 'Goldwyn'. But even as a successful Hollywood producer Samuel Goldwyn never quite managed to get to grips with the English language, as countless 'Goldwynisms' – apocryphal or not – prove:

Every director bites the hand that lays the golden egg.

Who wants to go out and see a bad movie when they can stay at home and see a bad one free on TV?

We have all passed a lot of water since then.

A verbal contract isn't worth the paper it's written on.

The reason so many people showed up at Louis B. Mayer's funeral was because they wanted to make sure he was dead.

Going to call him 'William'? What kind of a name is that? Every Tom, Dick and Harry's called William. Why don't you call him 'Bill'?

Yes, my wife's hands are very beautiful. I'm going to have a bust made of them.

Why only *twelve* disciples? Go out and get thousands!

If you can't give me your word of honour, will you give me your promise?

From the rails of a liner leaving for Europe, to friends on the quay:
*Bon Voyage!*

# <u>Very Interesting . . .</u>
# <u>But Stupid</u>

Arte Johnson used to deliver his catchphrase on *Rowan and Martin's Laugh-In* as a German soldier peeping through a fern. The show had a dozen or more catchphrases. *ITMA* had getting on for forty.
Test your knowledge of catchphrases.
The answers are on pages 89 and 90

With which entertainers do you associate these:

**1**

Can you hear me, mother?

**2**

I'm in charge.

**3**

Before your very eyes.

**4**

Right' monkey

**5**

The day war broke out.

**6**

I wanna tell you a story.

**7**

Hello, my darlings.

**8**

Now here's another fine mess you've gotten us into.

**9**

Oh, calamity.

**10**

Just like that.

In which shows were these catchphrases used?

**11**

Give him the money, Barney.

**12**

Ee, it was agony, Ivy.

**13**

I only asked.

**14**

I'll give it five.

**15**

I think the answer lies in the soil.

**16**

Seriously, though, he's doing a grand job.

**17**

Not a word to Bessie.

**18**

And now for something completely different.

**19**

Oh, get in there' Moreton.

**20**

It all depends what you mean by . . .

# **Answers**
## Very Interesting . . . But Stupid

**1**

Sandy Powell.

**2**

Bruce Forsyth.

**3**

Arthur Askey.

**4**

Al Read.

**5**

Robb Wilton.

**6**

Max Bygraves (he inherited it from people doing
impressions of him . . .).

**7**

Charlie Drake.

**8**

Oliver Hardy.

**9**

Robertson Hare.

**10**

Tommy Cooper.

**11**

*Have a Go* (Wilfred Pickles referring to the producer, Barney Colehan).

**12**

*Ray's a Laugh* (Mrs Hoskin, played by Bob Pearson).

**13**

*The Army Game* (Bernard Bresslaw).

**14**

*Thank Your Lucky Stars* (Janice Nicholls, member of a pop jury).

**15**

*Beyond our Ken* (Kenneth Williams as Arthur Fallowfield).

**16**

*That Was The Week That Was* (various characters. Ned Sherrin, the producer, says it was only uttered half a dozen times).

**17**

*Much Binding in the Marsh* (Kenneth Horne).

**18**

*Monty Python's Flying Circus.*

**19**

*Educating Archie* (Robert Moreton).

**20**

*The Brains Trust* (C. E. M. Joad).

# <u>Great God!</u>
# <u>This Is An Awful Place</u>

So said Captain Scott of the South Pole. The following
quotations – complimentary or otherwise – are all
about places.
Where do they refer to? Who said them?

The answers are on page 94

**1**

The shortest way out of _____ is notoriously a bottle
of Gordon's Gin.

**2**

One has no great hopes from _____. I always say
there is something direful in the sound.

**3**

Very flat, _____.

**4**

The Great Wen.

**5**

If you are lucky enough to have lived in _____ as a
young man, it stays with you; for _____ is a
moveable feast.

**6**

Four thousand holes in _____. And though the holes
were rather small, they had to count them all.

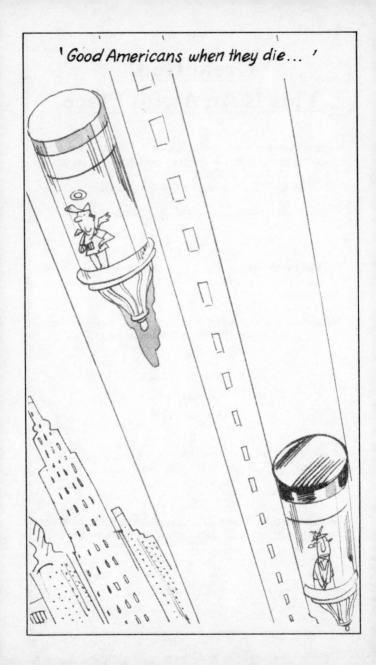

## 7

_____ is like eating an entire box of chocolate liqueurs at one go.

## 8

Home of lost causes, and forsaken beliefs, and unpopular names, and impossible loyalties!

## 9

Good Americans when they die go to _____.

## 10

And when bad Americans die they go to _____.

# **Answers**

## Great God
## This Is An Awful Place

**1**

Manchester. William Bolitho.

**2**

Birmingham. Mrs Elton in *Emma* by Jane Austen.

**3**

Norfolk. From Noel Coward's *Private Lives*.

**4**

London. From William Cobbett's *Rural Rides* (a wen is a wart, a lump, an excrescence).

**5**

Paris. From Ernest Hemingway, *A Moveable Feast*.

**6**

Blackburn, Lancashire. From the song *A Day in the Life* by Lennon and McCartney.

**7**

Venice. Truman Capote. (Robert Benchley once cabled Harold Ross of *The New Yorker* from Venice : 'STREETS FULL OF WATER. PLEASE ADVISE.')

**8**

Oxford. From Matthew Arnold, *Essays in Criticism*.

**9**

Paris. Thomas Appleton.

**10**

America. Oscar Wilde.

# 𝔚𝔞𝔰𝔥𝔦𝔫𝔤𝔱𝔬𝔫 𝔓𝔬𝔰𝔱

SPECIAL EDITION

# EXPLETIVE DELETED

## The Wit and Wisdom of Richard M Nixon.

You won't
have Nixon
to kick
around any
more.

*To reporters,
on failing to
become
Governor of
California,
1962.*

This certainly
has to be the
most historic
telephone call
ever made.

*To the first
men on the
moon, 1969.*

This is the
greatest week
in the history
of the world
since the
Creation.

*When they
came back
from the moon.*

I don't give a
shit about
the lira.

*23 June 1972.*

I am not a
crook.

*17 November
1973.*

# Ars Long<u>a</u>,
# Vita Sackville-West

## Music and musicians

Wagner is the Puccini of music.

> *Beachcomber (J. B. Morton).*

I liked your opera. I think I will set it to music.

> *Beethoven to fellow composer.*

The greatest composers since Beethoven.

> *Richard Buckle on the Beatles.*

There are only two things requisite so far as the public is concerned for a good performance. That is for the orchestra to begin together and end together. In between it doesn't matter much.

> *Sir Thomas Beecham.*

I could eat alphabet soup and *shit* better lyrics.

> *Johnny Mercer on a British Musical.*

## Actors and acting

She ran the whole gamut of emotions from A to B.

> *Dorothy Parker on Katherine*
> *Hepburn (adding that another actress*
> *kept upstage of Miss H. 'lest she*
> *catch acting from her'.)*

It made me feel that Albert had married beneath his station.

> *Noel Coward on an inadequate*
> *portrayal of Queen Victoria.*

Ears too big.

> *Verdict on Clark Gable's first screen*
> *test.*

Let my people go!

> *Lenny Bruce half-way through*
> Exodus, *the lengthy film about the*
> *founding of modern Israel.*

## Art and artists

The portrait is a very remarkable example of modern art. It certainly combines force with candour.

> *Churchill, on being presented with his portrait painted by Graham Sutherland. Lady Churchill's criticism took a more practical form. She ordered it to be destroyed.*

My god, they've shot the wrong person!

> *James Pryde, at the unveiling of a statue to Nurse Edith Cavell.*

## Critics and criticism

The characteristic sound of the English Sunday: Harold Hobson barking up the wrong tree.

> *Penelope Gilliatt.*

Asking a working writer what he thinks about critics is like asking a lamp-post how it feels about dogs.

> *Christopher Hampton.*

It seems to me that giving Clive Barnes his CBE for services to the theatre is like giving Goering the DFC for services to the RAF.

> *Alan Bennett.*

## Self-criticism?

The purpose of satire it has been rightly said is to strip off the veneer of comforting illusion and cosy half-truth. And our job, as I see it, is to put it back again.

*Michael Flanders of Flanders and Swann.*

Nothing happens, nobody comes, nobody goes, it's awful.

*Samuel Beckett*, Waiting for Godot.

It is as good as having a Government licence to print money.

> *Lord Thomson of Fleet in the early days of commercial TV.*

All my shows are great. Some of them are bad. But they are all great.

> *Lew Grade.*

I cried all the way to the bank.

> *Liberace on his reaction to adverse criticism. Now he says he owns the bank.*

# <u>Kinquering Congs</u>
# <u>Their Titles Take</u> – 3

Where are the titles of these films taken from – apart,
that is, from any books they may be based on?

The answers are on pages 106 to 108.

**1**
Kind Hearts and Coronets.

**2**
Days of Wine and Roses.

**3**
Gone with the Wind.

**4**
None but the Brave.

**5**
Twilight's Last Gleaming.

**6**
Paths of Glory.

**7**
Splendour in the Grass.

**8**
Ill Met by Moonlight.

**9**
Tender is the Night.

**10**
Mean Streets.

**11**
Go West, Young Man.

**12**
Lilies of the Field.

**13**
Behold a Pale Horse.

**14**
Deadlier than the Male.

# Answers

## Kinquering Congs
## Their Titles Take – 3

**1** 'Howe'er it be, it seems to me, / 'Tis only noble to be good. / Kind hearts are more than coronets, / And simple faith than Norman blood' – Tennyson, *Lady Clara Vere de Vere*.

**2** 'They are not long, the days of wine and roses' – Ernest Dowson, *Vitae Summa Brevis*.

**3** 'I have forgot much, Cynara. Gone with the wind' – Ernest Dowson, *Non Sum Qualis Eram*.

**4** 'None but the brave deserves the fair' – Dryden, *Alexander's Feast*.

None but the brave

**5** 'Oh, say, can you see by the dawn's early light, / What so proudly we hailed at the twilight's last gleaming?' – Francis Scott Key, *The Star-Spangled Banner*.

**6** 'The boast of heraldry, the pomp of power, / And all that beauty, all that wealth e'er gave, / Awaits alike th'inevitable hour, / The paths of glory lead but to the grave' – Gray, *Elegy Written in a Country Churchyard*.

**7** 'Though nothing can bring back the hour / Of splendour in the grass, of glory in the flower' – Wordsworth, *Ode (Intimations of Immortality)*.

**8** 'Ill met by moonlight, proud Titania' – Shakespeare, *A Midsummer Night's Dream*, II.i.

Ill met by moonlight

Splendour in the grass

The paths of glory

**9** 'Already with thee! Tender is the night' – Keats, *Ode to a Nightingale*.

**10** 'Down these mean streets a man must go who is not himself mean; who is neither tarnished nor afraid' – Raymond Chandler, *The Simple Art of Murder*.

**11** 'Go west, young man, and grow up with the country' – Horace Greeley, based on J. B. L. Soule.

**12** 'Consider the lilies of the field, how they grow' – St Matthew vi.28 (the Sermon on the Mount).

**13** 'And I looked, and behold a pale horse: and his name that sat on him was death' – Revelation vi.8.

**14** 'For the female of the species is more deadly than the male' – Kipling, *The Female of the Species*. This is one of a remarkable number of phrases that Kipling gave to the language: 'white man's burden', 'somewhere East of Suez', 'he travels fastest who travels alone', 'the widow at Windsor', 'flannelled fools', and 'East is East and West is West, and never the twain shall meet'.

# **Thought for the Day**

Would you rather be in the light with the wise virgins
– or in the dark with the foolish ones?

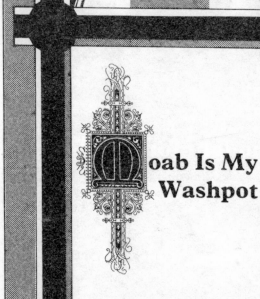

# Moab Is My Washpot

*Psalms lx.8 and cviii.9.*

Seldom is a quotation given more prominence than when it is the text for a sermon. It is perhaps spoken twice at the beginning and once at the end. Whether what is said in between has any connection with it is, of course, quite another matter – memorably demonstrated by Alan Bennett in his *Beyond the Fringe* sermon.
He took as his text a scrambled version of Genesis xxvii.11:

And he said, my brother Esau is an hairy man, but I am a smooth man.

Listen out for sermons based on the following:

Moab is my washpot; over Edom will I cast out my shoe.

*Psalms lx.8 and cviii.9.*

My beloved put his hand in by the hole of the door, and my bowels were moved for him.

*Solomon v.4.*

And it came to pass that he fell off the seat backward: for he was an old man, and heavy.

*1 Samuel iv.18.*

Go up, thou bald head; go up, thou bald head.

*2 Kings ii.23.*

Isn't God a shit!

*Randolph Churchill, while reading the Bible from cover to cover in response to Evelyn Waugh's bet of £10 that he could not do so.*

I have spent a lot of time searching through the Bible for loopholes.

*W. C. Fields.*

# **Better Left Unsaid**

Although he was not a politician, Lieutenant-Commander Tommy Woodrooffe was one of the first men to appreciate broadcasting's enormous potential for helping you put your foot in it – for allowing you to say things you would later regret and which would haunt you to the end of your days.

Describing the illumination of the Fleet at the Spithead Review in 1937, he said:

> At the present moment, the whole fleet is lit up . . . when I say 'lit up', I mean lit up by fairy lamps.

Naturally, everyone concluded that Woodrooffe was himself 'lit up' as the result of too much hospitality from his former shipmates on board H.M.S. *Nelson*. But he denied this. 'I was so overcome by the occasion that I literally burst into tears . . . I had a kind of nervous black-out. I had been working too hard and my mind just went blank.'

Here, on the following pages, are some further memorable moments.

During the Three-Day Week in 1974, Energy Minister Patrick Jenkin had an energy-saving idea. He was photographed using his electric razor by candlelight, and added:

People can clean their teeth in the dark.

In March 1966, John Lennon of the Beatles gave a newspaper interview in which he said:

Christianity will go. It will vanish and shrink. I needn't argue about that. I'm right and I'll be proved right. We're more popular than Jesus now.

The remark lay dormant for several months but when the Beatles paid a visit to the United States it was reprinted and caused an outcry. Lennon subsequently had to withdraw it.

In July 1957, Harold Macmillan said:

You've never had it so good.

He was echoing a US presidential election slogan from 1952 and although the context makes it clear that the remark was intended as a warning and not as a complacent boast ('What is beginning to worry some of us is "Is it too good to be true?" Or perhaps I should say "Is it too good to last?"') the phrase dogged him thereafter.

Harold Wilson, January 1966:

The cumulative effects of the economic and
financial sanctions [against Rhodesia] might well
bring the rebellion to an end within a matter of
weeks rather than months.

Ian Smith, March 1976:

I don't believe in black majority rule ever in
Rhodesia . . . not in a thousand years.

Edward Heath acquired two hostages to fortune within
the space of a month before becoming Prime Minister
in June 1970. On 5 May he addressed the Franco-
British Chamber of Commerce in Paris. Looking ahead
to the enlargement of the EEC he said that this would
not be in the interests of the Community:

Except with the *full-hearted consent of the
Parliament and people* of the new member countries.

This statement (written, incidentally, by Douglas
Hurd, a Heath aide) was seized upon later by those
seeking a referendum on EEC entry.

The phrase which haunted Edward Heath most,
however, was one that never even passed his lips. A
press release made available at a Tory press conference
contained the promise that a Conservative
Government would:

*At a stroke* reduce the rise in prices, increase
productivity and reduce unemployment.

Walter Annenberg, US Ambassador to the Court of St James went to present his credentials to the Queen in 1969. Unfortunately for him a TV crew was hovering at his elbow making the film *Royal Family*. So millions were able to hear the peculiarly orotund remarks he thought appropriate for the occasion. When asked by the Queen about his official residence he admitted to:

Some discomfiture as a result of a need for elements of refurbishing.

President Gerald R. Ford was noted more for physical than verbal ineptitude – but only by a narrow margin. In December 1975 he proposed a toast to Anwar Sadat with the words:

The President of Israel!

He probably scotched his chances of re-election in 1976 during one of the TV debates with his challenger, Jimmy Carter, by declaring that:

There is no Soviet domination of Eastern Europe.

In the same campaign, Carter gave an interview to *Playboy* magazine and said:

I've looked on a lot of women with lust. I've committed adultery in my heart many times. God recognises I will do this and forgives me.

The American electorate, perceiving a useful working relationship with the Almighty, let Carter off.

In 1961, before becoming Prime Minister, Harold Wilson said:

I myself have always deprecated . . . appeals to the Dunkirk spirit as an answer to our problem.

But – lo! – within months of taking office in 1964 he was saying:

I believe that the spirit of Dunkirk will once again carry us through to success.

In his TV address after the devaluation of the pound in November 1967, Harold Wilson said:

From now on the pound abroad is worth 14% or so less in terms of other currencies. That doesn't mean of course that *the pound* here in Britain, *in your pocket* or purse or in your bank, has been devalued. What it does mean is that we shall now be able to sell more goods abroad on a competitive basis.

A year later Edward Heath asked Wilson whether on reconsideration he would still have made the remark:

As to the accuracy of what I said, the answer is, Yes. But recalling the warning of Rudyard Kipling,

*If you can bear to hear the truth you've spoken,*
*Twisted by knaves to make a trap for fools . . .*

I might have had second thoughts.

# Like The Curate's Egg – 2

More scrambled quotations for you to go to work on.

The answers are on pages 122 and 123.

**1**

That first careless rupture.

**2**

Gone to that country from whose Bourne no
Hollingsworth returns.

**3**

They are rolling up the maps all over Europe. We shall
not see them lit again in our lifetime.

**4**

All women dress like their mothers, that is their tragedy.
No man ever does. That is his.

**5**

An honour is not without profit, except in your own
country.

**6**

A rose by any other name as sweet would smell –
a rhododendron, by any other name, would be much
easier to spell.

**7**

The money that men make lives after them.

'Absinthe makes the heart grow fonder'

**8**

Absinthe makes the heart grow fonder.

**9**

If you have ears, prepare to shed them now.

**10**

It is a far, far butter thing.

**11**

When I hear the word 'vulture', I reach for my revolver.

**12**

At my back I often hear / Time's winged chariot
changing gear.

**13**

A bachelor never quite gets over the idea that he is a
thing of beauty and a boy for ever.

# **Answers**

## Like The Curate's Egg – 2

**1** 'That's the wise thrush; he sings each song twice over, / Lest you should think he never could recapture / The first fine careless rapture!' – Browning, *Home-thoughts, from abroad*.

**2** 'Death / The undiscover'd country from whose bourn / No traveller returns' – Shakespeare, *Hamlet*, III.i. (scrambled by Beachcomber).

**3** 'The lamps are going out all over Europe; we shall not see them lit again in our lifetime' – Sir Edward Grey, 1914, and 'Roll up that map [of Europe]; it will not be wanted these few years' – William Pitt the Younger after the battle of Austerlitz (scrambled by Alan Bennett).

**4** All women become like their mothers, that is their tragedy. No man ever does. That is his' – Wilde, *The Importance of Being Earnest* (scrambled by Alan Bennett).

**5** 'A prophet is not without honour, save in his own country and in his own house' – St Matthew xiii.57 (scrambled by Michael Flanders).

**6** 'What's in a name? That which we call a rose / By any other name would smell as sweet' – Shakespeare, *Romeo and Juliet*, II.ii.

**7** 'The evil that men do lives after them. / The good is oft interred with their bones' – Shakespeare, *Julius Caesar*, III.ii. (scrambled by Samuel Butler – before death duties).

**8** 'Absence makes the heart grow fonder' – the proverb (scrambled by Oscar Wilde).

**9** 'If you have tears, prepare to shed them now' – Shakespeare, *Julius Caesar*, III.ii.

**10** 'It is a far, far better thing that I do, than I have ever done; it is a far, far better rest that I go to, than I have ever known' – Charles Dickens, *A Tale of Two Cities* (scrambled as a slogan by Dorothy L. Sayers in *Murder Must Advertise*).

**11** 'When I hear the word "culture", I reach for my revolver' – words usually attributed to Goering.

**12** 'But at my back I always hear / Time's wingèd chariot hurrying near' – Marvell, *To His Coy Mistress* (scrambled by Eric Linklater).

**13** 'A thing of beauty is a joy for ever' – Keats *Endymion* (scrambled by Helen Rowland).

**Famous
Last
Words**

The story is told of the relative of a dying man who – eager to record his last words for posterity – bent her ear down to catch his latest breath only to hear him say, 'Boo!' Last words are not something you can have a second stab at and only a few manage to go out with a memorable or appropriate saying on their lips:

Get my swan costume ready.

> *Anna Pavlova, affirming that even* in extremis *the show must go on.*

I shall hear in heaven.

> *Beethoven, optimistic on two counts.*

Mozart!

> *Mahler. For technical reasons Mozart was unable to reciprocate.*

The sun is God.

> *J. M. W. Turner.*

I've had eighteen straight whiskies. I think it is a record.

> *Dylan Thomas (he had probably drunk only four or five).*

## Could have done better

I am Heinrich Himmler.

*Heinrich Himmler (no really).*

I want my lunch.

*J. Paul Getty.*

Have you brought the cheque-book, Alfred?

*Samuel Butler.*

# Write your own epitaph

If after I depart this vale you ever remember me and have thought to please my ghost, forgive some sinner and wink your eye at some homely girl.

*H. L. Mencken.*

He never used a sentence where a paragraph would do.

*Huw Wheldon.*

On the whole I'd rather be in Philadelphia.

*W. C. Fields.*

## Trying too hard

My exit is the result of too many entrées.

*Richard Monckton-Milnes.*

Ah well, I suppose I shall have to die beyond my means.

*Oscar Wilde, on being told the cost of an operation.*

## False alarms

You should have known that it was not easy for me to die. But, tell me, were my obituaries good?

*President Makarios, 1974.*

I'm super-jew!

*Lenny Bruce, leaping from a window but only sustaining a broken leg.*

## Drawing peacefully to a close

No, it is better not. She would only ask me to take a message to Albert.

> *Disraeli, when it was suggested to him that he might like a visit from Queen Victoria.*

What's the question?

> *Gertrude Stein, when asked by bosom-pal Alice B. Toklas, 'What's the answer, what's the answer?'*

## Alternative versions

1  I have been an unconscionable time dying and I hope you will excuse it.
2  Don't let poor Nellie starve.

*Charles II has both these sets of dying words attributed to him.*

1  How is the Empire?
2  Gentlemen. I am sorry for keeping you waiting like this. I am unable to concentrate.
3  Bugger Bognor.

*George V runs to three sets – the last in response to a courtier who suggested that the King would soon be well enough to visit his favourite seaside resort.*

# Epitaphs

A man of much courage and superb equipment.

> *On Brigham Young, the Mormon leader, who died leaving seventeen or more wives.*

Ars longa, vita brevis.

> *On Thomas Longbottom.*

Under this sod lies another one.

> *On Anon.*

# Appendix*

**Princess Anne (Mrs Mark Phillips)** (1950–   )
  One flew over the cuckoo's nest. *Attrib.*

**Mark Antony** (*c.* 82–30 B.C.)
  The biggest asp-disaster in the world. *On the death of Cleopatra*

**John Logie Baird** (1888–1946)
  I think I will just turn over and see if there is anything on the other side. *Last words*

**Mrs Beeton** (1836–65)
  I think I am just about done now. *Last words*

**Alexander Graham Bell** (1847–1922)
  Dead, dead . . . and never called me mother.
  *Last words*

**Charles Dickens** (1812–1870)
  Compliments to the chef, but I think the sauce was a little brutal this evening. *Oliver Twist*, chap. 2

**General Franco** (1892–1975)
  Yes, we have no *mañanas*. *Last words*

**W. G. Grace** (1848–1915)
  Congratulations on your overnight stand. *To Casanova*

**Ernest Hemingway** (1898–1961)
A farewell to arms. *Of the Venus de Milo*

**Herod Antipas** (?–*c*. A.D. 40)
Sorry, dear, brains are off. *To Salome when she asked for John the Baptist's head on a platter*

**Lenin (Vladimir Ilyich Ulyanov)** (1870–1924)
I was born under a squandering Tsar. *Attrib.*

**Napoleon I (Napoleon Bonaparte)** (1769–1821)
C'est magnifique, mais ce n'est pas la gare. *On arriving at Euston instead of Waterloo*

**William Pitt** (1759–1806)
Oh god! I think I have just eaten one of Bellamy's veal pies. *Last words*

**Sir Walter Ralegh** (*c*. 1552–1618)
Be of good comfort, Master Ridley. We shall this day light such a candle by God's grace as I trust shall never be put out. *On introducing tobacco to England*

**Richard III** (1452–85)
A hearse, a hearse . . . my kingdom for a hearse! *Last words*

**Marquis de Sade** (1740–1814)
    This is going to hurt me more than it hurts you.
    *Last words*

**Henri de Toulouse-Lautrec** (1864-1901)
    Come down and see me some time.

**Madame Tussaud** (1761–1850)
    Once I was waxing—now I am waning. *Last words*

**Queen Victoria** (1819–1901)
    The Empire's decision is funereal. *Last words*

# Envoi

Go! And never darken my towels again!

*Groucho Marx*, Duck Soup.

# INDEX

*Also from Nigel Rees in Unwin Paperbacks*

# Graffiti Lives, OK

Over 300 graffiti from every part of Britain and also
from other corners of the globe are presented in the
collection. Bawdy, brilliant, obvious and obscure, the
graffiti are as unpredictable as they are varied. Sexual,
political, literary and metaphysical subjects have been
drawn from many situations (loos, fly-overs, subways,
bridges); and their sites range from the Bodleian
Library in Oxford, via a Wall in Alaska, to the Ladies'
in Chorlton-cum-Hardy.

# Graffiti 2

Just when you thought it safe to walk past a wall or
visit a Public Convenience again, comes a fresh
collection of the graffiti you might encounter. Over 400
*new* examples of graffiti that provide superb
entertainment have been brought together in this
second collection by Nigel Rees to be published in
**September 1980**.

# Very Interesting . . . But Stupid!

How do catchphrases come about? Why do they exert
such a hold over people? In this collection drawn from
the world of entertainment, Nigel Rees brings together
the catchphrases that 'caught on'. At their best,
catchphrases live on, evocative of an era and of past-
pleasure, enriching the language. The best probably
came about by accident, but, as this book shows,
quite a few were deliberately concocted and were
seized upon by the audience. *Very Interesting . . . But
Stupid!* will jog memories, recall past enjoyments
and provide fascinating footnotes to a part of show
business history.
**July 1980.**

*When they were talking about

1. His autobiography
2. The Press
3. A policeman's job
4. *Lady Chatterley's Lover*
5. Power
6. *Saturday Night and Sunday Morning*